eXplore

AUSTRALIA'S FIRST PEOPLE

an Ancient Journey

R.T. Watts

KNOWLEDGE
BOOKS AND SOFTWARE

9

T0358073

Teacher Notes:

This fascinating book explores the journey of Australia's First Nations people over 60,000 years ago during the Ice Age. Students can explore how land bridges made Australia accessible for many other countries and learn more about the original migration and language development of the First Nations Peoples of Australia. The impact that colonisation had on these people and their languages is also touched on and provides an avenue for further discussion.

Discussion points for consideration:

1. How did the First Nations people make their way to Australia? Where did they come from? What challenges did they face?

2. Tasmania's First Nations people were decimated within 70 years of colonial occupation. Discuss these actions further.

3. How did the First Nations people explore Australia's vast inland regions? How did they survive and communicate? What challenges did they face?

Sight words, difficult to decode words, and infrequent words to be introduced and practised before reading this book:

Queensland, Western Australia, South Australia, different, mountains, Celsius, swimming, freezing, deserts, explorers, Wiradjuri, origins, Tasmania, temperature, Europeans, colony, languages, Palawa, dugongs, Truganini, observations, Indigenous, material, conditions, protection, comfortable, wilderness, settlement, preserve.

Acknowledgement of the First Nations' People: We acknowledge the Traditional Owners of country throughout Australia and recognise their continuing connection to land, waters and culture. We pay our respects to their Elders past, present and emerging. kilometres, rescue, information, understanding.

Contents

1. About the First Peoples

The First Nations people came to Australia 50-60,000 years ago. This is a very long time ago. This is such a long time that it is hard to compare with other peoples.

There are no other places on Earth where the same people have stayed in the one place for so long. The First Nations people have been in Australia a long time.

Who were these people and how did they get to Australia? DNA of the First Nations people shows that they have ancient African origins.

Where did they come from? When the First Nations people first came to Australia there were land bridges.

The sea-level was not as high as it is today. There were land bridges north to Papua New Guinea. To the south there was a land bridge to Tasmania.

People could have moved along the coast in Asia. The people would have been used to being near the sea. Canoes would be used for travel.

Scan these QR codes below for videos on the DNA history of the First Nations people.

2. Pathways to Australia

The sea crossing to Australia would have been less than 100 km. This means they could have paddled to Australia's islands and coast in 24 hours. The people would have known about the land to the south. They could feel the wind and heat from Australia.

The other way to Australia was the land bridge from Papua New Guinea. The people could have walked down into Australia. The people would follow the coast and get their food from the sea.

The First People came down from Asia over 60,000 years ago. This would have been when they first entered Australia.

The people would have moved south, possibly by walking along the coast. The coast had food and was easier to walk than going inland. There would have been less food and water inland. The people came from the north and came down the coast of Western Australia and Queensland.

The people ended up in Tasmania and South Australia. The whole of the inland was explored and settled by the First Peoples moving up the rivers.

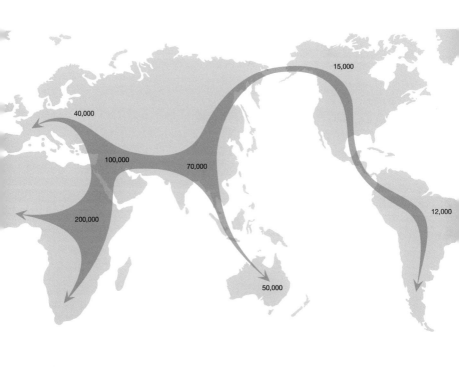

40,000

15,000

100,000

70,000

200,000

12,000

50,000

Australia was very different 60,000 years ago. The sea was a long way out from where it is now. The climate was very different.

The climate was colder. There were many mountains with ice and snow. To travel across these mountains would be very hard. To explore inland from the coast would be tough. They would have had to cross areas that were cold and dry, with less food around.

Australia had many deserts as well as forests. The cold period had some parts that were warm but generally it was colder. If you think of the temperature in winter, it would have been about 5 degrees Celsius colder than that.

3. Australia in the Ice Age

Australia was in an Ice Age during the early period of First People's entry to Australia.

This was the last Ice Age that Australia has seen. The Earth started to warm again about 10,000 years ago. By about 5,000 years ago the Earth had warmed a lot and the waters were rising.

The climate was changing, and some areas were getting warmer and wetter. This was the start of the warm period which we are still in today.

Many of the mountain ranges had ice along the top. The central part of Tasmania was covered in hundreds of metres of ice.

The early explorers along the coast and inland noted what they saw. In the southern cold parts along the coast, the First People were swimming in the freezing waters. The water and air were too cold for the explorers.

So how did they stay warm? It seems that they were covering their bodies in seal fat and grease. This extra layer helped keep them warm.

4. First Nations of Australia

Studies show that the nations of people in Australia formed a long time ago. It was over 50,000 years ago.

All areas of Australia had First Nations people. This included the deserts, mountains and islands. There were no parts of Australia which did not have people living there. When the Europeans arrived in Australia they said they had "discovered" it. This is like going to a beach, and seeing someone's towel and saying it is mine as no one has stopped me.

17

The Europeans thought the land was empty. They thought they could change the land as it was wild. They changed the land to suit the sheep and cattle. Wild animals were kept out or killed.

The people on the land before the colony did not have a right to land. The Europeans said they did not own the land.

The Europeans built a colony so that people could use the land. They did not see all the work the First Nations people did on the land, because they did not farm like Europeans. First Nations people cared a lot for their country, which is why they kept it for 60,000 years.

5. Crossing the Land Bridge to Tasmania

Tasmania was cut off from Australia when the sea levels rose. The sea levels rose over 90 meters about 5-6,000 years ago. Before the warm period, Tasmania was joined to Australia.

People could walk down through the land bridge to Tasmania. The First Nations people of Tasmania spoke different languages to that of the mainland. There were about 10,000 First Nations people in Tasmania. These people were called the Palawa people.

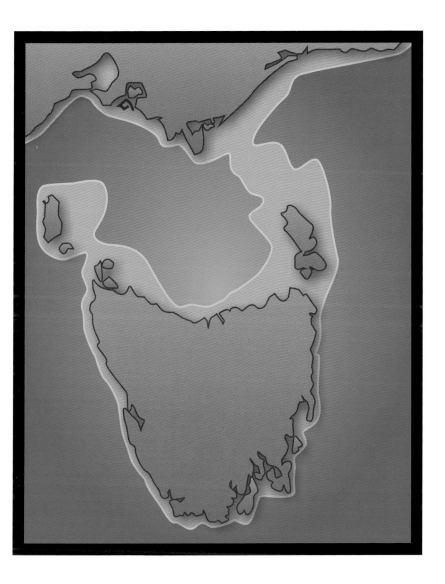

The Palawa First Nations people had plenty of food to eat. They would hunt large mammals like whales or dugongs for their meat.

If whales washed up on to the beach, they could also be used for food. The people did not go too far off shore in search of food. It would be difficult to hunt whales as they were very big.

In the northern part of Australia, dugongs were hunted in shallow waters with spears. They were able to be speared and caught. Turtles could be caught by diving off a canoe.

NATIVES ATTACKING SHEPHERDS' HUT.

The last person of the original Tasmanian First Nations people died in 1876. It is said that Truganini was the last full-blood Tasmanian.

We can only guess how many First Nations people died in Tasmania. Based on observations, the numbers would have been high.

Tasmania is a richly forested land and the number could have been tens of thousands. In less than 70 years, the First Nations full-blood people of Tasmania had all been killed or had died from different illnesses.

This terrible period is now gone but not forgotten. Respect for past troubles is still given.

Australia 10

Australian Women

Truganini 1812-1876

25

On the Australian mainland, things were not any better. Settlers wanted the land for sheep and cattle. The land was to be used for farms. This meant houses, barns, fences, roads and new animals.

The land was no longer there to hunt animals for First Nations People. This led to wars across Australia with the First Nations People.

Attacks on settlers' farms happened across Australia. This led to settlers killing many Indigenous people. As their food supply ended, the Indigenous people had to survive by working for the settlers.

6. Shelters

The shelters used by the First Nations People changed based on available materials and conditions. Shelters for a warm and rainy place were different to shelters for a cold and windy place.

Across Australia, First Nations People built different shelters. In the rainforests in the far north of Australia, the two most important things were high rainfall and insects. The shelters were built to stop heavy rain. The door was very narrow, and smoke was used to kill the mozzies.

In the desert regions of Australia, the shelter was built to stop wind and sand. The shelter was built to have shade from the hot Sun, and to stop the desert winds and blowing sand.

The shelter was built to have protection. The shelter was made of a wall of thick tree branches and tied together to stop the wind and sand. This also gave a lot of shade.

Rock shelters and caves were used across Australia. These were away from winds, bad weather, rain and snow.

Fires were lit in these rock shelters and people could be comfortable and sleep.

The First Nations people would move over their country and stay in spots they knew. Each place had food and somewhere to stay. They would repair the shelters, or use the cave when hunting or fishing in that area.

7. Moving Inland

After the coast of Australia was settled by First Nations People, they moved inland over 50,000 years ago.

The best way was to follow the rivers and creeks. This would allow them to get food and water from the river.

It is said that these rivers were the pathways inland for the First Nations People. Many of the names of the people are related to their place within the waterways. The Wiradjuri people are the people of the three rivers.

As the people moved inland, the nations of people formed along the rivers and plains. These were places for hunting and access to water. This was all they needed to live well in these areas. There was plenty of water and food from fish in the rivers, and kangaroos and other animals on the plains. Plant foods were also found in the soil and in the trees.

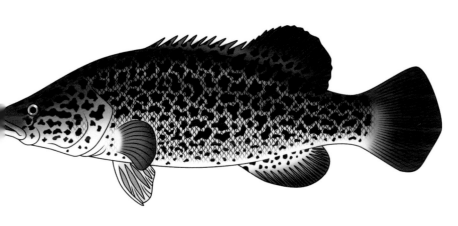

The inland deserts seemed a very harsh place to live. But the First Peoples lived in Australia's deserts for many thousands of years. The people had skills to live well.

The last group to be found were people in the 1980s who lived in the desert. They were called the Pintupi Nine. These were a group near Alice Springs. When the people were checked by a doctor they were found to be in perfect health.

They stayed in the wilderness for the whole of their lives up until 1984. They put their spears down and walked into the centre. They watched the strangers in their lands but stayed away until they finally were talked around and came in.

39

These First People lived in the desert off many types of animals.

They feared the white men and hid when they saw cars driven by white men. They had worries about the spirit man who lived close-by and wanted to stay away from the settlement.

Food was easy to get. "I would spear mala [kangaroos], emus, pussycat, rabbits, snake… It was easy to catch them. I made my spear sharp with a limestone rock."

41

8. Nations Form and Languages change

The languages of the First People all came from a common language, but this was a long time ago. Later there were over 300 different languages spoken by the First Peoples. Each of these languages was a nation of people.

Many people could speak the languages of other First Nations. When they came to the border of their nation they could talk with the other nation and make sure they stayed friendly to each other. This was important to stop wars starting and get permission to travel across their land.

PUNAPA
DARKINYUNG WARRANGO
WAJARRI YANGMANIC
PUNKALLA JARRAKAN
PAMA—NYUNGAN
PITJANTJATJARA
WAGIMAN
NYUL NYULAN
GNALCHTWARLIN
KUKUBERA

Word Bank

Indigenous

language

African

canoes

coast

entered

Queensland

Western Australia

South Australia

different

mountains

Celsius

Europeans

swimming

freezing

deserts

islands

explorers

Tasmania

Truganini

Wiradjuri

temperature